# MY CHILD AND GOD

# *My Child and God*

*Religious Education in the Family*

# *Anne Marie Zanzucchi*

**new city press, new york**

Published in the United States by New City Press
the Publishing House of the Focolare Movement, Inc.
206 Skillman Avenue, Brooklyn, N.Y. 11211

© 1978 by Città Nuova Editrice, Rome, Italy
Printed in Hong Kong
Translated from the original Italian edition Mio Il Bambino e Dio
by Lenny Szczesniak

1st printing: July 1978
2nd printing: January 1979

Nihil Obstat: Reverend Martin S. Rushford
Diocesan Censor

Imprimatur: Francis J. Mugavero, D.D.
Bishop of Brooklyn

Brooklyn, New York    October 23, 1978

**Library of Congress Card Number: 78-52599**
**ISBN 0-911782-31-1**

## CONTENTS

1. What religious education is, and how it comes about   7

2. The foundations of religious instruction for those under ten years of age   39

3. The beginning of religious observances, the first contact with the Church   55

4. The religious perspective of daily events: the meaning of suffering   83

# Introduction

*"I came to the realization," a young mother said, "that for a long time I'd been worrying only about my child's physical health. I tried to prevent colds; I recorded his weight gains on a chart. His health became a kind of fixation. The fact that he had a soul never entered my mind. Nor did I realize that he has an interior life — one that was just beginning, one which, accordingly, needed to be nourished with great care.*

*"Just in time, I realized that I was making a mistake. I learned that, to care for his soul and help him grow, I had to become less superficial myself."*

*The following pages offer parents of young children some practical ways of doing what this young mother did: helping their children grow in their relationship with God and with other people; and becoming less superficial themselves. The book is not intended as an exhaustive inquiry into the theory of religious education of young children. Rather, its methods are rooted in reality — in the experiences of the author and of a group of parents whom she interviewed. They speak honestly and freely about difficulties and the success they have encountered in introducing their children to God, to prayer, to Jesus and Mary, to Scripture, to examination of conscience, to the sacraments, to suffering and death.*

*The author sees religious education as "the patient and sensitive work of developing children's inherent sense of the supernatural, the divine, the transcendent." Thus, she emphasizes that parents must provide a personal witness of Christian life, and that the family is a crucial influence in forming what she calls the child's "evangelical mentality."*

*Faith, she insists, is faith in the love of God; and this faith is communicated to the child through daily Life. "If the child is asked to respond to the love of God as it is manifested in nature, in external events, and in the events of each day, he is being encouraged to model his life on the pattern of Love itself."*

*The "method" of religious education explored through the experiences of these parents, then, teaches the child both to recognize God's love and to love in response. This love-focused view brings fresh light to the teaching and learning of doctrines, observances, and moral laws — light for both parent and child. "The child gets used to making love the measure of all things," the author says.*

*The goal? "To form a human being who believes in the love of God, and who has learned to love."*

chapter one

**What Religious Education Is and How it Comes About**

# The Development of a Man

I don't think we can speak of religious education as a division of education all by itself. It enters into the total formation of man as man. When we get the body into shape, when we feed the intelligence and the will, when we accustom our children to self-control and orderliness — then we are establishing the foundations for their possible experiences of the transcendent, the divine.

I remember one of our family's first hikes together. It was a few years ago, in a mountainous region. We set outselves the goal of reaching a shelter far up in the mountain side.

After just one hour of climbing, my husband and I could see different reactions in the children. Our eight-year-old, who was quick and agile, was always in the lead. He would gladly have gone on by himself if we had let him. Our ten-year-old, instead of walking straight along the path, would stop now and then, puff a bit, and ask, "How much farther? Can you see the shelter yet? Give me some water." So I tried to make the younger one understand that the mountain could be dangerous and that he had to be prudent; and the older one that he had to move on with resolution and confidence.

Half way there, one of the children began to have a nose-bleed. We were quite upset at first. "What are we going to do now? It's too far to go back and still far from the shelter!" We stopped and tried to keep calm. A little cotton ball, a little rest, and we were on our way again. As we went on, we began to realize that the climb was more strenuous than we had thought - and we had our little ones with us! At certain places we had to move single file, holding on to one another. It was no longer possible to suggest that we turn back. No one would have agreed. We would never have admitted defeat or shown ourselves unfit for the situation. We went on, overcoming fatigue and difficulties, and we reached the shelter, exhausted but happy. As we rested, we noted that the children were enchanted by the rocks and by the succession of mountains off toward the horizon. They listened to the silence of the mountains at that height. Then they met two impressive guides — strong, silent, and peaceful men.

When we returned that evening, my husband and I shared our impressions of the day. We both thought that the children experienced the happiness that comes from overcoming something with sacrifice, that they surely felt the importance of such human virtues as prudence, courage, and perseverance. What most struck us, however, was the sense of the sacred that each of us felt in our hearts. It stemmed from the beauty of nature, which said even to the littlest of us, "What must God, who created all these beautiful things, be!"

Everything that day — the fatigue, the joy, the risk,

and the conquest — made us feel the zest of being human. The atmosphere surrounding our evening prayers was unusually beautiful. The children thanked God with spontaneity, for they found — we could sense it — a deep personal relationship with him.

Some time later, a mother told me this. "When I care for my children's health, by getting them to take up some sport, when I try to open their minds to current events and to history or point out to them something beautiful in nature, when I give them a push at the right moment and in the right way, even when I try to have them dress well, I realize that what I am doing is helping them to develop as men. At the same time, I feel I'm establishing a foundation so that right now, and in a deeper way in the future, they can make their own the things of God. That's because the more man is man, the more his relationship with God will be deep, conscious, and responsible. Undoubtedly, my difficulty is in knowing how to harmonize the various aspects of life to the child. I realize that an excess in caring for health or in encouraging sports is just as detrimental to his development as being careless about health or being blind to laziness."

We might also consider the goals expressed by a father of three young children: "In order to help my children find their places in the world that surrounds them and to give them the right orientation toward life, I've tried to keep them in touch with reality from the time they were very little. I've urged them to discover for themselves the underlying meaning of everything. In this way, I told myself, if God is truly present in all of creation, with his order and his laws and his harmony, it's impossible that my children will not meet him. Moreover, this meeting will come about — I should say, *especially* come about — through contact with people. Our part is to help them make this contact a deep one, not a superficial one. For example, when a visitor is expected at home, a mother and father can talk to their children about this person. They can speak of his talent, his good qualities; about the relationship that links him to the family.In other words, they can make sure that the meeting will have a certain depth and not remain superficial. I read of a theologian who held that human encounters of this kind pave the way for meeting with God." For that matter, we might well remember here what Jesus said, "Whatever you do to the least among you, you do to me." So it seems clear that in meeting with people, we meet with him and, thus, with God.

### Religious Education in Itself

Even though religious education is part of the total education of the child, it still has its own characteristics.

In religious education there are three essentials: God, who gives the faith; the child, who freely receives it, and who always has the possibility of rejecting it; and the parents, who with the support of religion teachers, must be the channel between God and the children. Here is how one father saw his role: "I've tried always to keep in mind that God wants to have a personal and direct relationship with my children. I've tried to be careful not to interfere in this relationship, but only to foster it. I absolutely do not have the capacity to infuse the faith in my children, no matter how hard I might try."

"How often," acknowledged a mother, "we think we *own* our children! We look at them and treat them as 'things' belonging only to ourselves. Perhaps because we've found the meaning of life in our faith, we expect that it will be the same for our children. We force them into religious practices that they often don't feel comfortable with. What we're trying to do is instill faith in them by force. We have to resist this. I know that I must remind myself to have the greatest respect for my child, for God wants to communicate directly with him. I can become an obstacle to my child's faith, to his love for God, if I stick myself between him and God."

It's true that we parents have to cultivate the greatest respect for our children and for the message we are transmitting. The message is, after all, the Word of God — not our word!

We know that the faith is infused in our children at Baptism. Transformed at the core, they become children of God and followers of Jesus. Well then, do we really have to educate them at all? Actually, with Baptism, God gives children the capacity to believe, but it's still necessary for this capacity to be transformed into a free and personal act of faith. This is where our effort and our responsibility comes in. We have to help our children to "exercise" their faith. Otherwise, it will remain as a seed that does not grow, that in time dries up and dies.

13

## Does Religious Education Infringe upon Freedom?

There are those who will say, "If at a certain age our children rebel against the religion that we've given them, it means that we didn't leave them free. It means that we forced something on them and that they shook it off as soon as they could."

Others say, "If we provide a religious upbringing for our children from their infancy, this makes an impression on their subconscious that cannot be removed, so that all their future choices will be conditioned by the fact that we parents decided to make Christians of them."

Certainly it can happen (in fact, most often it does) that religion is poorly presented to children. But to say that it shouldn't be presented at all doesn't seem right to me. I find a confirmation of this right in the Gospel. If Jesus had wanted to preach only to adults, he would have kept the children away from him. Instead, he preferred to have them close to him and he spoke with great love of the little ones "who believe in me."

Moreover, Jesus reproached the disciples when they tried to keep the children away so they wouldn't disturb him. "Let the little ones come to me." "Let," he said, which implies that the children experienced a spontaneous natural attraction for Jesus.

In another place Jesus says, "If you do not become as these little children, you will not enter into the Kingdom of Heaven." This sentence is usually interpreted on a moral plane. Children are innocent, pure of heart, and we have to imitate them and become pure and uncontaminated like them. This is true. Yet I've always liked to think that Jesus also intended to say that we adults, complicated and rationalistic as we are, have to acquire the simplicity and immediacy with which the "little ones" accept the idea of God. Children "comprehend" God; they contain him in their souls. We don't take away their freedom if we help them discover him.

"On the other hand, what sort of freedom can a baby have? He doesn't have the use of reason, and therefore he doesn't have freedom either," rightly observed a father of three. "It's more correct to say that he is destined to be a rational and free man, but at the moment he is not yet so. Did we ask our children just after they were born if they wanted to eat? And then later, did we ask them if they wanted to go to school? Their choices were certainly conditioned by us parents. We love them, and we choose what we think is right for them. But the children are not denied their freedom because of this. It is our job to guide them, to lead them toward freedom. Each child has a hunger for God. He has been created in his image and likeness, and he is naturally inclined to search for and find a relationship with God. This is why we felt from the time our children were little that we had to transmit our faith to them, first with our lives and then with words too. We knew we had to help them as much as we could to know God."

It's natural for parents to pass on to their children all aspects of their total human life. It's logical, therefore, that if our greatest treasure is life understood as a relationship with God, then we'll pass this treasure on to our children — even without speaking of it, because it's a reality, "And for that matter," someone pointed out, "whatever attitude we have concerning religion, don't we still form our children according to it, whether we want or not? If we *live* as Christians, we show them a *fact* that will certainly influence their lives. If we don't live as Christians, we'll still influence them, but in the opposite way, of course."

In any case, a time comes for everyone without exception when they have to make their own personal choice of God. (This is one of the most convincing proofs that despite everything, our children's freedom remains intact.) It might come at twelve or at fifteen or at twenty years of age. It's the moment when every person asks himself more or less explicitly, "Who is God for me; What is my relationship with him?"

"I've seen it happen with my children too," said a mother of seven young adults. "When they got to be eighteen, nineteen, twenty — those ages of difficult choices — they always made a personal acceptance (which might have been a rejection) of the religion they saw us profess from the time of their birth. I have to say, however, that this choice of theirs, made at the young adult age when a really true act of faith can blossom, was preceded by other choices. I've seen my children make acts of love to God at seven and eight years of age, and perhaps before that. Maybe not all the necessary elements of a "conscious and full act of faith" were there; yet they certainly made acts of love for God. They were small (and sometimes big) choices of the God with whom they were beginning to dialogue."

Actually, many parents have discovered from

experience that by helping their children to *live* what they were learning from religion, they were also helping them with the successively more serious choices they had to make in growing up. In trying to translate the Gospel message into life, both parents and children personally experienced what in theological language are called the fruits of the Spirit: joy, peace, serenity, a sense of spiritual fullness. So it was logical that this positive experience would confirm the truth of the religion they had been learning all along, for the worth of the plant is known by its fruits.

## What Is It That Educates?

### a) *The Witness of Life*

"I think that more than any other thing, the witness of our lives educates our children in religion." This is what a mother of three said in a letter to me.

I also think that we affect our children by what we *are* even more than by what we do.

A member of a French religious order who is particularly involved in family problems said, "Education is a transfusion of life." There is no way around it. To demonstrate a living faith is a formidable undertaking.

For parents who really want to educate their children, a personal conversion is indispensable. Some might rightly object, "Don't we already have the faith? How can you say that we have to be converted?" I'll let a mother reply: "Every morning I feel that I have to renew my life, my commitment, my love for God and for everybody. Naturally, I don't try to do this just for the sake of my children. I do it out of an interior need, in order to live fully each new day with all its unknown joys and sorrows, and in order to make use of each reality I have before me in the best way possible. I do it out of a deep desire to converse with God through the events of the day. This is why I make a conversion daily. At the same time, I feel that by doing this I can hope to educate my children."

Actually, how many of us parents — we who so readily call ourselves Christians — have become so well "established" that we are fossilized in a static faith? We need a dynamic faith, a continuous effort, an incessant tension toward a greater love. Then religious education will be a natural result of what we do. It will stem from life and give life. There will not be one who only *gives* and one who only *receives*. Everything will be an exchange, a "growing," an educating of each other together.

"I have to say that I was not the one who helped my children in their religious life, but they helped me," a mother with an admirable sense of humility said to me. "In order to prepare them for a life in which religion was not an abstraction but a reality, I had to do for them what no one had done for me. Not only did I have to live a life consistent with my faith, but I had to study and know more deeply the elements that made it up. For example, I wanted to know the meaning and value of the Mass better, and to discover the beauty and depth of Scripture. In particular, I was fascinated by the greatness and the poetry of the psalms. The more I enriched myself with these things, the more I was able to transfer to my children an interest in and love for them too."

A father of four boys added this: "If a person is convinced, he can transmit this conviction. Otherwise he can't. At least I'm not going to ask my children to believe something that I myself deep down do not believe."


b) *The Family Environment*

I don't think it's always easy these days to assess statements of this kind. In fact it's natural to wonder how many of these people who want to educate their children in religion really believe in the relevance of their faith. We may wonder if they are convinced that in developing a man in the true sense of the word, it is necessary to strive from the first days of his life to insure that the supernatural and natural values in him are integrated and in harmony. We know that such harmony is made possible by the incarnation of Christ, in which the human has been eternally united with the divine. Starting from this conviction, while remaining mindful of the difficulties found in our environment, we can capitalize on the fact that in the first years of life the child lives almost exclusively in contact with the family. Therefore the atmosphere of the family in which he finds himself is most important for his religious education.

Here is the witness of a father and mother in this regard: "When we were first married, our plan was to help our children develop as men, as Christians. But when we looked at the world around us, we were discouraged. Society condoned things that were exactly the opposite of the Gospel message. Hate, indifference, attachment to wealth, ambition, eroticism. We then realized the importance of the family. When we get right down to it, in the very first years of life, children live twenty-four hours out of twenty-four with us parents, in the family environment. All those human and religious values that we would like the world to show our children can in some way be shown to them by us. And even more important than our limited personal virtue, we can give them our mutual love. This would create an atmosphere that is warm with love and full of serenity in the home. In fact, (and this is for us and for many families a consoling discovery) we could create a climate that was 'sacred' with religiousness — not made of words or external actions but of life. 'Where there is charity and love, there is God,' the early Church had sung, because of a true experience of this, and it can be had today too. This means that God can be present every moment — when we are working, when we are resting, when we are sitting down to eat or study, even when we are joking and laughing. That's if we care for one another.

"What did we do? We did not increase our prayers. We intensified the love between us. And this has been our most important effort in these first years of marriage — to know each other better, to understand and accept the personality, the limits of each other." Some will object that it's almost impossible to have this "constant" love between husband and wife. And they're right. But the important things is that we *want* to love one another and that we make an effort to grow in love.

An opinion held by many psychologists is quite consoling. They think that no matter how serious the defects of parents may be, no matter what their incapacities are, the love they have for their children and for each other constitutes a reality that their children can feel. By living out the family experience — by not running away from it but by embracing the sacrifices it requires — parents give witness to their love, and this gives their children the security they absolutely need for their emotional development. In this way, parents encourage an exchange of love, even if it is somewhat confused or sprinked with a lot of selfishness. And so their children can begin to experience some dimension of love — and that is the substance of religion. Naturally, if this love is refined and purified and modeled on the Gospel, the children will spontaneously grow toward a Christian life.

Moreover, Jesus said, "Where two or more are united in my name, I am there in their midst." Thus, a mother and a father who really try to love one another, who try to be "one" through the sacrament of Matrimony, offer to their children the possibility of living in contact with God. And where there is Jesus in a community, no matter to what degree, there is a portion of the Mystical Body — of the Church. It would not be surprising, then, if the children, having had a vital contact with the Church, would come to know it and love it, and would inadvertently grasp the communitarian and social aspect of Christianity.

## When and How Religious Education Begins

We've said that religious education enters into the large area of education in general. Now, psychologists and educators maintain that the action of education begins very early, already in the period of pregnancy. In my view, the same can be said regarding religious education.

It is known that the bond between the mother and the child she carries in her womb is not a purely physical one. It is also affective and spiritual. The mother is responsible for providing for the child not only physical nourishment, but also — and especially — love, peace, and serenity. Moreover, a mother at the first awareness of her pregnancy — assuming it is wanted or accepted well — experiences within herself a desire to be better, more patient, more serene. She has this desire for his sake, for the little one's sake. She feels that, in some way, everything she does has an influence on the child.

Obviously many mothers will at this point object, "Okay, all that is true, but we're not perfect. What are we going to do?" I also expect to be asked how they can avoid the physical, moral, and spiritual traumas that are beyond their control. I think an experience of one mother provides an appropriate answer to these objections. "I have five children; so more than once, while waiting for one or another of them to be born, I have had moments of serious difficulty and deep sorrow, over and above the daily difficulties of pregnancy. I recall being in a state of very strong tension for days on end while awaiting my third child. I was afraid this intense suffering would cause some sort of trauma for my baby. But what was I to do? I certainly didn't have the power to eliminate all the sufferings of life. Then, all of a sudden, I received a kind of light. No, I couldn't eliminate them. But I could try to bear them as well as possible. So I tried to accept that suffering, all the time confident that God loved me and my child. I acquired a new strength and a serenity in confronting that stressful situation. Above all, I felt that this new attitude of mine served as a filter between the suffering and the child. The child, now fourteen, is the most serene and balanced of them all."

Then too, (though I won't go into it at length here) we should remember that the baby is influenced when a mother tries to live in "friendship" with God. Unfortunately, the less we concern ourselves with these things, the less we'll understand them and, above all, the less we'll value them. Yet since moral disorder, hate, and malice do lead to negative consequences for the baby, how great must be the positive effects stemming from the "presence of God" in the mother, from her life of grace! An expectant mother once confided to me with a radiant air of certainty: "Can you believe that Jesus in the Eucharist upon entering in me (or better, I entering a little more in him) would not have an influence on this child that is an integral part of me?"

Then, when the child is born, religious education will continue to take place for months and months without his conscious participation in it.

What is most important in this period, is the manner in which the child comes to know his parents. This knowledge will have an indelible influence on his future idea of God. And in fact, with the love that binds them and with the love they have toward the baby, they manifest *Love*, which is God. Their love is nothing more than a ray, a reflection, a participation in the love of God. Unconsciously, but in a deep way, the baby comes to know Love. Christian psychologists state that if a baby is not able to enjoy and take advantage of the love of his parents, of the infinite manifestations of this love, the idea of God he will have as an adult will often be inadequate and deformed.

On the one hand, the goodness of God, his continuous loving presence, is shown to the baby through the goodness and the presence of the mother. On the other hand, the security and the strength of God is shown through the father.

God, however, is not simply an enlargement of the father and the mother. He is the real "Other." How then will the baby be able to grasp the reality of this superior Being?

I don't think we have to worry too much about this. It's enough that we live our lives as Christians with simplicity, without ostentation and without undue modesty.

This is what a couple told me: "Whenever we could, we always prayed together. It was natural for us to get on our knees for a few minutes in the evening to thank God for the benefits of the day and to unite ourselves to him in prayer. At first our baby, although in the same room, slept on and wasn't aware of anything. One evening when she was a little more than a year old, she was awake for some reason or another. I remember that pulling herself up a bit she looked at us through the rungs of her crib. She repeated this a few times in the following weeks. She was probably a little puzzled to see us talking, but not to each other because we weren't looking at one another. Also, from her high chair she had seen this same manner of talking, with the same seriousness and composure, when we said a short prayer before eating. When she was able to understand, I think I told her in very simple words, 'We're speaking with God.' I must have repeated this same sentence a number of times to her in that period. For I realized what is rather well known, that a small child doesn't need explanations so much as he needs simple and essential statements."

Naturally, this is only an example. It's not necessary to speak about God so early to babies. The important thing is that the "religious" attitude of parents be simple, spontaneous, and sincere. Life speaks for itself, and the baby will intuit the presence of the Person his parents are turning to. Also, we don't have very much to teach infants, especially in the early months. It's only a matter of uncovering the image of God that is already in them. A father told me: "I know, not just from reading, but especially from observing it in my children, that the capacity for God is a primordial possibility of man. The need to experience him is 'natural' in us. It is the law of kinship that ties us to God and that we have impressed within us from birth."

## The Starting Point: God-Love

One of the first things that I've told each of my children about God (and I think it was accepted by them) is that "God loves us. God loves you, he loves dad, he loves mom, he loves everybody." Our smallest child believes me because he knows that I always tell him the truth. He also knows what "to love" means. That's because many times I spontaneously say to him, "Do you know that I love you?" He smiles, delighted. He understands. And when someone asks him how much he loves his father, he throws open wide his arms, as if to say very, very much.

The child thus begins to understand that this Person to whom his parents turn is good, and he loves the way his mommy and daddy love. The child knows that this Person helps and protects him and everyone he knows.

Here is what a widowed mother of two daughters had to say to us on this topic. "The first reality that I presented to my babies was the reality of God-Love. I didn't do this just once. I emphasized how much the love of God, present in our lives, gives us. For example, I showed them how God, through their grandfather, gives us what their father would give, and even more. I showed them how God had prompted so many parents to be near us and to be full of concern for us. I always try to act in such a way that even the loss of their dad is not seen by them as something negative. Even in the moment when their father passed away, God could not have done other than love us. In thinking of their daddy, who is already with God because he was good and was ready for heaven, we too are preparing ourselves to possess with him a happiness that no one can take away."

"At a certain moment in my life," a father told me, "by some kind of grace the conviction that God is Love, that the word *Father* with which we address him each day in the Our Father is a *reality*, hit me like lightning. My whole life was changed. It was natural for me to tell everybody — particularly my children — about this discovery of mine. Soon we became accustomed to look for and discover in the circumstances of life the continuous love of God for us. There were so many occasions when we experienced it! The words that I was able to say to them were substantiated by facts! In short, I feel that only if children see their parents accept all that comes about as coming from the hands of God, will they be able to orient their lives in a religious direction."

One thing is certain: our children want authenticity. My husband and I became aware of this during the period of youth protests, and we are more and more aware of it living side by side with them. They reject all that is formalistic, and, unfortunately, along with the structures they often reject the substance too. Maybe, however, they have never known the substance; that is, maybe they have never experienced it. We must always give the substance of religion, from the very first years — especially in the very first years. From our interviews with other parents, we find that the central idea in their efforts of religious education is God-Love. This is true in educating children of all ages.

I won't dwell on this topic here because I'll be able to recount various experiences about it as we go along.

Certainly, from infancy the child should feel himself wrapped up in this Love. And as a logical consequence (helped along by us), the child will soon understand that Love asks for love in return. He will begin to love and become active in love. His love for God will not be something sentimental, made only of words; but it will be immediately concrete and real.

For such a child, from his very first years, loving God will mean loving one who is near.


### The Love of God in Nature

I did not concern myself too soon about telling my children of God the creator, but the transition was very simple. The most important thing was that they "know" love as a result of seeing it close to them in those who were always with them.

I recall what happened to me with one of my children when he was two or three years old. We were in the mountains, and one evening we came in rather late. I had undressed John and was putting him in bed when I glanced outside. It was a marvelous night. A full moon shone against the dark heavens. I took my baby to the window and pointed out the moon to him. He stared at it with a look of wonder. He had never seen it before. "God made the moon and put it in the sky to give us light at night." I said to him. Well, that scene surely remained impressed on him because later, when he saw the moon, he would say, "God made it."

Not long ago, another of my children, who likes to sketch the things that impress him, drew and colored a daisy, a tulip, a bunch of grapes, three stems of grain, and four ants on a large sheet of paper. Above each he put a little yellow cross. "What does the cross mean," I asked him. "It means that they are all good things created by God." One day he asked me, "Mommy, did God create this cabbage?" I answered, "Yes, but we don't know how he created it. We know that everything came from him because he loves us and wants to give us beautiful and useful things" Later on I tried to develop these first considerations about nature through conversation and reading.

One must keep in mind that the small child thirsts for experiences from life. Things that awaken his sensitivity will make the greatest impression on him. For this reason, it is very important to help him to observe, to listen, to see those things that he doesn't notice at first. We have to awaken in him a sense of wonder, a sense of the marvelous. The things that make him wonder will remain impressed on him.

Infancy is an age in which to awaken the love for nature as it is, without giving sermons; nature speaks to the infant by its very existence. Of course, we need a little imagination on our part in order to excite in them a sense of wonder. This would mean taking them up to the mountains at sunrise or to the sea on a windy day. Or, more simply, it could mean helping them discover the marvels of a world so small that it can't be seen be the naked eye or so big that it can't be contained in our view. Many times I've watched my husband surrounded by the children, squatting down on the ground to watch the movements of ants or of an earthworm, or to observe the colors and details of tiny, almost invisible flowers!

Usually, when one shows aspects of nature to children, an atmosphere of silence and recollection is created, like an enchantment. I think that the discovery (for them it's a real discovery) of the beauty, the harmony, and the force of nature, helps them to come in contact with God, who has impressed something of himself in created things. What I mean to say is that for them, these are moments of contemplation.

Then, little by little as they grow older and pick up clues from the ordinary little things of daily life (such as the blooming of a geranium and the changing of the seasons) or from the less ordinary (such as spending some days by the sea or in the mountains), it is possible to show them the love there is in nature. The difficulty here is that first of all we adults have to be able to see these things in this way.

I recall one Sunday when we were in a meadow outside the city. The children had been playing at full speed. Perspiring and hardly able to catch their breaths, they came over to rest under an oak tree where my husband and I were talking. I don't remember exactly how, but looking at the oak, the hills, and the river that flowed a short distance away, we began talking about nature. It seemed to us that everything was love, that each thing was a gift for someone or something. It was a discovery made together, and it was a silent invitation to each one to search for his own "place of love" within reality. That evening I was able to observe in my children a greater effort to love one another.

I remember speaking about this topic to a friend of mine who then told me two experiences she had with her child.

"We were in the country staying with a friend. In the morning we went out into the garden. The ground was soaking wet because the evening before there had been a storm. There was a rich fragrance. I noticed a rose bush climbing along a wall. A bud that had probably bloomed during the night, still swelling and full of moisture, was now basking in the sun. A bee landed on it and began to draw out the nectar. You know how it happens sometimes — something that you're seen many times suddenly has an impact on you and makes you reflect. 'See that?' I said to my boy. 'The water of yesterday his been a gift for the rose. It drank and bloomed. And now the rose receives the bee who draws out the nectar. And he will make the honey that you like so much. You can see it. Even without our intending it, we all live one for the other. God has bound us — men and things — together with love.

"Another time, we were taking a stroll along a walk in the public gardens that are near our home. I was holding Luke's hand and we were walking slowly. It was autumn. The leaves of the tall chestnut trees were falling from the branches little by little and they fluttered in front of us before coming to rest, dried out and golden, on the ground. 'Have you ever asked yourself.' I decided to ask, 'why the leaves fall in Autumn?' 'No,' he answered pensively. 'I have,' I continued, 'and I've come to this conclusion. In summer it's hot from the burning sun and a little cool shade to walk or rest in is really a delight. But in the winter it's cold, and we want to get as much of that sun as we can. The leaves fall and leave the branches dry and bare. The sun passes through the branches and we can take advantage of it. Hasn't God thought of everything?' 'It's really true,' he said, 'God is good. He really loves us a lot.' "

Obviously, this mother wasn't trying to give a theological discourse. Still, it's undeniable that the awareness of some relationship existing between nature and man (especially if the awareness is immediate) does invite us to discover the love and wisdom of God beyond the external appearances of things and and coldly scientific ways of approaching them.

## Being Active in Love

I said previously that "Love calls forth love." Now, the will of God is the design of love that he has for each one of us. It gives a new dimension to our lives and our duties. But we can say this to our children only if they feel a true relationship with God as father; only if they are convinced of his love. If they have this, they can then return it. How can they return it? "Not the person who says, Lord, Lord, is the one who loves me, but the person who does my will," Jesus cautioned us. Thus, the only answer to the love of God is to freely choose to do his will. But one must be very careful!

There is a commandment that is especially fitting for us parents. "Do not use the name of God in vain." I mean it fits in this sense: too often we are tempted to drag God in front of our children in order to make them do things they should do. Many times I've had to bit my tongue so that I wouldn't impose my will on one of my children — in the name of God! This would happen sometimes when one of them didn't want to study. I would say to myself, "But no! *I* have to do the will of God, without expecting it from them. They'll do it if they see me doing it, not because I've forced them to do it." Then I would start giving them a hand, maybe to search out a book, or look up a word in the dictionary. Little by little, they would get going again by themselves.

Otherwise it could happen that out of the habit of hearing the name of God always linked with obligations, they would end up not understanding anything. All the beautiful things would be obscured and they would grow up with a feeble faith — if they hadn't already rebelled altogether. Certain things have to reveal themselves within a young person; he himself has to feel what he is supposed to do and how he has to conduct himself.

To the person who asked him what the greatest commandment of the Law was, Jesus answered, "To love the Lord God with your whole soul, with your whole mind, with your whole strength," and he added, "The second, then, is similar to the first: Love your neighbor as yourself." This is the crux of the matter. We cannot claim to have brought our children to know God and to love him if we haven't taught them to love their neighbor.

From their earliest years, our children have understood almost instinctively that "being good" meant "caring for" those around them. This came about even before we were able to explain with words that it was necessary to love, and why it was necessary to love. Maybe they were helped by the fact that my husband and I tried to maintain an attitude of concord, of love, not only between us, but with relatives, friends, and acquaintances. We tried to be open to everybody. I don't mean to imply that the children were angels. In fact I recall very well certain battles my daughter had with her cousin Johnny when they both were two years old. Each wanted the toys of the other. This resulted in pushing, screaming, and crying. But still, there were many times when she would also come smiling to me and say, "I like Johnny!" in her own way she wanted to underline her first acts of love toward her cousin and her victories over her selfishness.

By trying not to become pedantic — in other words, by doing, rather than by teaching — we were always able to help them give themselves to others with generosity, and not to close up within themselves.

Just as the child is "made" to find God in his life and to have a relationship of filial love with him, so too he is a member of human society and has by nature a bond with all other men.

Just as we parents feel a duty to help them find God, so too we feel that we have to help them establish a relationship with all those persons they will eventually find near them through the years, and even with humanity as a whole.

"When there are little arguments among my three children," a mother told me, "I try to remind them that everything done out of love will not pass away, while those things that are not love are like smoke. When Jesus will call us at the end of our lives and ask us what we have done, only the things we have done out of love will have value. Everything else will count as nothing. I've always told the children that Jesus was born to teach us how to become like him. And the more we're able to love, the more we'll be like him. When he calls us to him, he'll recognize us if we resemble him; that is, if we have loved. If we haven't loved, he won't recognize us. If he recognizes us, he will take us with him into Paradise. If he doesn't recognize us, there won't be any room for us in Paradise.

"My older child who is five years old," she continued, "has a kind of spontaneous inclination toward loving. So even if she gets into all kinds of trouble, she 'rehabilitates' herself because she easily starts to love again, to do things in order to please her mother or her brothers and sisters. On the other hand, she is a formidable preacher. Her little sister has a less flexible personality and finds it very difficult to make 'acts of love'. The older one will tell her very gravely and solemnly, 'Look. The only thing that counts is love. Everything else is smoke. If you don't get used to loving. Jesus won't recognize you . . . and when you find yourself before him in Paradise there won't be any room for you, do you hear? There won't be any room!' This kind of talk (apart from all the conclusions one can draw from it) does help the other one take some little steps which are in reality very big, considering how much effort it is for her to soften her rather stubborn nature. At times I really feel I'm observing the maturing of my children's personalities because love doesn't cancel out the self but directs it towards others and develops it in a social dimension."

This leads me to another consideration.

Children *must* express their personalities and *affirm* themselves, but, in their contact with reality, they run up against their own limitations. Some parents at times multiply these difficulties by repressing the personality that is just blossoming and by creating tense situations or even traumas. Others try to eliminate all obstacles for their children and give free sway to their desires. This, however, is going to the opposite extreme. There will always be limitations on the personality of the child, such as the typical limitation that comes from the presence of brothers and sisters. Actually, they contribute to his harmoneous development. An education in love seems to be the only solution to ensure that such inevitable limitations are accepted and are not merely endured. Love involves an act of the will, a free act that is thereby destined to develop the personality instead of suppressing and deforming it.

It is true that if children put themselves at the service of their neighbors and make an effort to love, they will find themselves and be happy. Someone told me a story that illustrates this.

"One day I had just returned from teaching school. I had hurriedly put on an apron and had just put a pan on the stove to prepare supper when my son came in. He flung his notebook on the table by the door, his jacket on a chair and flipped off his shoes. Then he came into the kitchen. 'Will you wash your hands and start to set the table?' I asked him after a quick hello. 'No!' he exploded. 'I'm tired. I don't feel like doing anything.' 'But listen,' I started up again, More gently this time, 'I was tired too. While I was walking home and stopping off to pick up some things for supper, I was so tired that the idea of coming home and preparing supper overwhelmed me. Then I realized that in cooking I could show my love for you and your dad, and this was beautiful. And now look. I made something that you like, and it's made me feel as if I've already rested.' 'Yeah, I know. You're saying this to get me to set the table!' Well, I heard him go off into the dining room and slam the door of the cabinet where we kept the tablecloth. In the kitchen too, while he was trying to take the dishes from the shelf, he made a lot of noise. I stayed quiet. The forks and knives began to fall on the table a little less noisily. Then, little by little, from the dining room I heard only some tinkling and shuffling of slippers on the floor.

"Finally, he came into the kitchen all smiles. 'You know, it's really true!' he exclaimed. 'While I was putting the tablecloth on the table, I was really angry. With the plates, a little less. With the forks and knives still less. And now that I'm finished. I'm really happy.' He stood on his tiptoes and gave me a kiss.

chapter two

# The Foundation of Religious Instruction for Those Under Ten Years of Age

## Sacred Scripture

If our intention is to educate our children in religion, and if the religion we want to present to them is Christianity, the best thing we can do is to put them in contact with God, with Jesus, through Scripture. God himself through his word will give them the fundamental principles of the faith. Sacred Scripture, therefore, will be the ultimate "textbook" of our children, even though it will be our duty to read and explain it to them.

"The one who educates," wisely remarked a friend of mine, "must be extremely careful not to impose a predetermined personality on the child, but to develop the child's own personality in its human-divine dimension. In this vein, I have seen how important it is to help my son love Sacred Scripture and the Gospels in particular. In fact, I began very early to read him daily passages from *The Bible for Children* or passages of the Gospels broken down into a language he could understand. I was glad to see that he liked these readings very much. He got quite excited over the Jews crossing the Red Sea. He was engrossed listening to the miracle of Cana. He himself would urge me almost every day, 'Mommy, read me the

Bible. Mommy tell me a parable.' And he didn't want me to explain the meaning. He preferred to discover for himself the teaching that Jesus wanted to give to man, and to him in particular."

The same thing happened to us. When Clare was three or four years old, we gave her an illustrated book of Bible stories adapted for children. Naturally, she couldn't read it by herself, so when I had a free half hour I sat down and read to her. Actually, more than read, I told her the stories. These were deeply intimate moments — calm and serene.

As I prepared myself to tell a Bible story, I noticed that in a certain sense I had to forget everything that I thought I knew; I had to make myself "one" with Clare and try to grasp what she was looking for. I had to take *her* into account — her age, her personality, her receptivity. She, not I, was to be the measure. It was quite consoling for me to discover that if I maintained this kind of attitude toward her, I succeeded in giving her even very profound things in a way that was simple, understandable, and also pleasant.

I soon lost the desire to have her understand a lot of things. Previously, I had acted as if her religious formation hinged upon how many ideas or narrations I gave her. But I realized that children often get indigestion from too much information. This doesn't mean that they are to be left to die of hunger! A happy medium is needed. I've seen that it's more important *how* rather than *how much* you give. For instance, I couldn't tell Bible stories in a cold impersonal manner, but had to participate intimately in what I was telling. As a result, I got into the habit of first reading a passage by myself. Often I read it in a regular adult Bible, along with the footnotes, with the intention of penetrating its meaning as deeply as possible.

It's not very easy to convey the significance of the Old Testament. There's the danger of making Sacred Scripture into a book of stories, of conveying to the children more the adventure and entertainment than the religious content. So I always tried to emphasize by means of the particular episode I was reading, the inner message of God. I wanted the reading to bring my child (and me too) into contact with the divine, with what God wants to tell us — people of the twentieth century — through an event that took place thousands of years ago. Moreover, in reading a passage, I took great care to distinguish clearly the supernatural from the magical. For example, when I spoke of miracles performed by Jesus, I tried to stress mainly his love, so that my child, right from the beginning, would not confuse Jesus with fairytale characters.

I did these things with my other children too, and I saw that they loved readings from the Bible. It made them especially happy to know that these accounts were true; that we were speaking of things that really took place. Sometimes they would interrupt me to make sure that it was really like that. And then often during the day one of them would burst out, "Tell us a true story!"

I think it's harmful to allow children to believe anything they will later learn to be false, such as the story of Santa Claus. An air of magic is created for the children as they learn to expect this old man who brings gifts. Then, when they learn that he is merely fiction, they may be inclined to think Jesus is a fiction too. In my opinion, magical things should not be fed to children if they are not made to understand clearly that they are only fictions and not true. Fortunately, little children are less easily fooled now, and already at three years of age, they often see through it all — although they may not let on, in order to get more gifts!

## The "Word of Life"

When we expose our children to Sacred Scripture, we have to remember the importance of helping them translate into life the things they are coming to know. "Only you have words of eternal life," Peter said to Jesus. And Christ himself, when speaking about himself, is very clear on this: "I am the way, the truth, and the *life*." So it's obvious that one cannot learn about the Word of God and hold it in esteem without feeling an obligation to live it, to put it into practice.

"To be sure that the things we read in the Gospels did not remain on the theoretical plane," a mother explained to me, "my husband and I chose a passage, a thought, some saying of our Lord, and we tried to help our child understand how to put it into practice. As it happened, his lively interpretations gave me the opportunity of clarifying many things touching a life based on the Gospel. One time, for example, we read together the passage of the Gospel that speaks about the vocation of the first disciples and ends with these words: 'and they left their nets at once and followed him.' I had explained to our son how he could put it into practice. 'Look,' I said, 'if you see Jesus in your mommy and daddy and grandparents, when they call you, you'll obey at once and leave aside what you were doing, without coming up with excuses. Do as the apostle did. They didn't say to Jesus, "Wait a while until we pull our nets to shore," or "Wait until we catch our fish." No, they followed him at once." Luke was somewhat at home with the idea that Jesus was in every neighbor — and hence, also in his mommy and daddy — I felt that he had been satisfied by this explanation. As a result of this conversation, I presumed he was more ready to overcome himself and obey without delay.

Some days later, however, while he was playing in his room and I was running the vacuum cleaner in the dining room, Luke called me. 'I'm coming,' I said to him, but I kept on working, thinking it might be better to finish first. 'Leave those nets right away,' he shouted from his room. I stopped the vacuum cleaner and went to him right away. He was very happy with this readiness — delayed though it was. But after listening to what he had to say to me, I stayed on to speak with him for a while. I explained how God entrusted to parents the job of raising the children he sent them, and how for this reason he gives them many graces. I explained that a daddy and mommy represent Jesus in a special way; and for this reason they are to be treated not only with the love we give to other persons, but also with the respect we would give when listening to Jesus. I saw that he understood this explanation well, and that it seemed logical to him."

Besides the formation of a new mentality patterned

on the Gospel, other effects come from putting the words of life into practice, especially in a large family such as mine. Most notably, our relations with each other have grown deeper. When the children were small, we would gather together in the evening before going to bed. We would tell each other some little detail of how we succeeded (or failed) in living the word of life. The children liked this, for they could tell their little experiences too. They liked it especially because in these moments, they felt equal to us — everybody was on the same level, in a fraternal relationship. Then, when they got older their sense of independence grew so strong that they felt it a restraint to gather together in the evening on a set schedule. So the occasion to meet as equals to communicate these experiences became unplanned — a moment at the table, perhaps, for an intimate moment together. They were shared with naturalness associated with things that are always true; they were never forced, always authentic.

It's surprising to see how children, being practical and concrete, can grasp the Gospel precepts so easily and apply them immediately to daily circumstances.

Here is a little episode a mother told me. "One morning while I was walking my child to school, we went into a bakery to buy something for his afternoon snack. In the store we met a little girl and her mother and another little boy we often took along to school with us. The little girl had a tendency to exert a sort of protective possessiveness toward the little boy, and always tried to draw him away from my son who was his friend too. So, when she saw us, she came over and said in a brusque manner, 'Louis is with us. We'll take him. Leave him alone." When we came out of the store, Luke was sulking. 'I can't stand her,' he blurted out. 'I know,' I conceded, 'It's not very nice when she acts like that. But you should not speak that way. Didn't you tell me that you wanted to love everybody?' 'Yes, but I don't like her!' 'I'm not saying that you'll like everybody,' I replied, 'But Jesus said to love your enemies,' All of a sudden he stopped in the middle of the street. He was wearing one of those school bags that you strap to your back. He put his hands on his hips and said, 'You're really something! You're like little Jack.' He was referring to his Jack-in-the-box that sprung up each time the lid of his box was opened. He went on, 'Everything I do or say, everything that happens, pop, a phrase of the gospel comes out of your mouth. It's really something! There's one for everything!' "

## The Life of the Saints

So far I've suggested that it's best if the first true stories told to children are taken from Sacred Scripture, in which the true protagonist is God. In the second place, we can also tell them stories of the saints. The saints are authentic Christians, people who have imitated Jesus. It is encouraging to discover them as normal people, with the same limits, defects, and instincts that we have and subject to the same temptations, yet able to live lives consistent with their faith. Children need someone to measure up to, someone with whom they can identity themselves. They need models. The saints can be these models.

Everything depends, however, on *how* we are able to present these personalities to them. One must depict these older brothers of ours in the right way, as men and women who have loved God. Yet because of a mistaken hagiographic tradition we are often accustomed to seeing saints as extraordinary, very unusual persons who are so unreal as to seem dehumanized. Children don't like this. They get bored because these saints seem to be too foreign to their world; or they become afraid in the face of the penances or the heroic deeds they performed. Children need authenticity. I remember being given a book about a saint when I was eight. I read it, but I skipped over all the descriptions and impressions (very sentimental, for that matter) and everything the writer added to make it seem like a novel. Indeed, I read avidly all the words and precepts reported to have been said by this saint. Today I still feel a special friendship with her.

When we consider the lives of the saints, we should give particular attention to the thrust with which they loved God and their neighbor. This is the glowing wake they've left behind them; it continues to enlighten us. Of course, it's necessary to put them in their historical setting. For example, St. Peter Nolasco, the founder of the Mercedarians, gave himself up as a prisoner to the Saracens in exchange for some slaves. Well, there isn't much slavery any more. However, there are certainly other kinds of slavery in our modern world, and we can bring that out. Children understand such examples right away.

We once went on a trip to Assisi. Some time before that, I bought a book about St. Francis and St. Clare.

I read it and so did my husband. Then, as we were visiting the city of St. Francis we told the children many details which they found captivating. For example, when we told how St. Clare left her home and family for an ideal, we reminded them of a person they knew who had done something similar. Then they were able to compare the two. The experience of St. Clare did not seem to be an unreal story out of the distant past but something current, something to be repeated today. Then we showed them the places (the actual places!) where St. Francis prayed, where he went for walks, where he wrote his *Canticle of the Sun* (they liked this very much because they were just beginning to love nature), where he hid from his father who wanted to take him back home, and so on. Naturally, we tried to emphasize God's presence in the life of St. Francis and God's love for him. But we were basically speaking of a man like us, who suffered and thought and ate and slept. There was heroism, yes; but a heroism that was possible because God's love was always watching over Francis, and Francis was always joyously responding with his love.

Through the lives of the saints, it is possible to give a Christian perspective to history and to many human events. For instance, the private and public life of St. Catherine — from her relationship with the Pope, the cardinals, the king, the military men, and the poor — a whole period of civil history, of the Church, and of humanity can be brought to life.

I'm beginning to realize what an enormous patrimony we have in the Church. Too often we do not know how to take advantage of it. Too often we make it seem so insignificant and irrelevant that our children reject it.

They especially reject it when, after we have told them something, we conclude by moralizing. We might think it our duty to tag a little thought on at the end; however, that is the way to ruin everything. We've given them something immense in itself and then we reduce it to the dimension of our own mentality and our own considerations. How often we've been told point blank at this point, "Okay, okay, we know all that." When we're eating, for example, and my husband and I are giving an account of something, the children are very attentive. In fact, if they have to get up and get the salt or something else, they ask us to wait a minute till they get back so they won't miss a word. But if we imprudently start commenting or drawing moral conclusions, there is a mass escape. In a few minutes, only the two of us are left at the table.

There's no avoiding the truth: children don't want things imposed on them.

## You Cannot Explain Everything

Children three or four years of age certainly cannot take up theology. This is the age at which they discover many realities, but not the age of connecting facts and making synthesis. It's quite useless to draw a theological picture for them — even a simple one. This would therefore exclude talking about the Trinity to little children, because there is the danger of giving them the idea that there are three Gods. The same thing goes for the subject of the Incarnation, which they will hear about later. There's no need to hurry.

And we should not give the impression that we can offer an explanation for everything. Actually, God is a mystery, and it's good that the children realize this. Frank said to me unexpectedly one day when he was five, "When I think that God is infinite, I, well, I just don't understand." Then he looked toward me expecting an answer. "You'll understand something more as you grow older, and especially as you try to love, but we'll never understand God completely," I told him.

A mother told me that she was able to communicate something of a sense of mystery to her child. "For some time, Luke had been asking me, at the most unexpected times, 'God made the world, didn't he?' 'Yes.' 'God made me, right?' 'Yes, but why are you asking me? Aren't you convinced?' 'I'm convinced, I really am, because neither the animals nor the stones nor man are made by themselves . . . . But one thing I don't understand. Who made God?' 'No one. God always was and he alone can do everything.' 'Yes, I know.' Still he remained pensive and dissatisfied. When he cut off the conversation, he seemed to be surrendering, resigning himself. He couldn't expect anything more from me. Later, however, perhaps while he was getting ready to crawl under the covers — in one of those warmly intimate moments that occur between a mother and her child — he started on the attack again: 'I just can't understand how God was able to make all things and make himself too.'

"I was up against that desire of children to contain everything within their own experience, to understand the core of things, to touch everything with their hands — the thing that makes them dismantle and destroy toys just to know how they're made. And I wasn't able to explain this 'beginning without a beginning.' Then one summer evening, we were at the seashore. We were standing on a terrace that looked out on a wonderful view. The sun was setting behind a low hill covered with trees. My boy was enraptured by the view. 'God really made some beautiful things!' he exclaimed suddenly. A little later, he started up the same old topic. 'But I don't understand . . .! Then I got an idea. 'Do you see how many things you can see from here? It's because we're up high. We don't have anything in front of us blocking our view, and you have good eyes. You don't need glasses. Yet, you are only able to see up to a certain point and not beyond that. For example, off in the distance in that direction is the city of Milan. You know that Milan exists, and I'm telling you that it's in that direction. But, even with your good eyes, you aren't able to see it. It means that your eyes are limited. It's the same with our minds. We think; we reason; we understand many things well — but not everything. There are certain big things that touch God — our heads cannot understand them. But they're still true, as true as can be. It's just that they're too big for us.' He was happy. I could see that this conversation had put him at peace. In his simplicity, he had grasped a sense of the mysterious. He understood what it means to say, 'It can't be explained.' "

This is not to deny that in their simplicity and spontaneity, children at times are able to intuit the truths of faith and, so to speak, also explain them —

to the point of helping us adults understand. Here is what a mother told me about this: "One day, my child (who was not yet four) left me breathless by an intuition of his that forced me to reflect for a long time. I was reading a passage of St. John that spoke of the mystical body. Johnny was playing nearby with his cars. All at once he said, 'Mommy, read louder.' I answered, 'Johnny, it's not a fairy tale. I didn't think it would interest you.' 'That's all right. I'll still like it.' To make him happy, and to show my confidence in him, I did what he asked. I read slowly and carefully. At a certain moment, Johnny stopped me and said, 'I get it mommy. Jesus in me, Jesus in you, Jesus in Sara [his sister], all Jesus!' "

chapter three

# The Beginning of Religious Observances
# The First Contact with the Church

## Prayer

For the first two years of our first child's life, when I put her to bed in the evening, I would make the sign of the cross. Of course she didn't understand what I was doing. She even may have linked the sign of the cross to that pleasant sensation she experienced in having me near her before going to sleep.

One evening when she got a little older she saw me and my husband praying; she stood up in her bed and tried to climb over the railing. We helped her out and she immediately knelt down next to us. At first she didn't say anything. She only imitated our attitude. She did this gladly because children like to imitate adults. Then she learned a few words of the Our Father and Hail Mary. We let her be, for we didn't worry about getting her to learn our adult prayers. Instead, little by little as she became more aware of God, we helped her say some short prayer to him that related to something she had been able to grasp, for example, "God, take care of daddy, mommy, and me." Then, when she began to grasp that God is the source of all things, she could say, "Thank you for all the beautiful things you have made." And after a beautiful day of vacation, she said, "Thank you for a beautiful day." Finally she was able to say, "You know that grandma is sick. Help her get well."

I think that these were her first true prayers. They were short but real conversations with God, based on a trust in him.

The first prayer that we taught our children was the Our Father. At first they learned it in an abbreviated form, in simplified words they would understand. Then they learned the way Jesus taught it to us. I felt that the first prayer of the child had to be directed to God the Father. Then later when they knew the story of Jesus and of Mary, it was natural for them to learn to say the Hail Mary in the evening.

Many mothers have told me instead that the first prayer learned by their children was the Hail Mary. Some parents speak of Jesus and his mother before mentioning God the Father to their children. Having some picture of them in their bedroom, the children recognize Jesus and Mary right away. I would once again stress that the important thing is not the prayer that they learn, but how they see it "said" by us.

Some would question whether or not it is good for the child, when he reaches a certain age (which naturally varies according to the ability and the interests of each one) to learn the "classical" prayers. I think it really is. I recall my own experience. Before putting us to bed, my mother gathered us children together (some of us were still very little) and she had us recite evening prayers. For me it was a true recitation, without any participation of my mind. It was too difficult to think of the meaning of all those words, which had become so familiar to me that they aroused no interest at all in me. Yet I have to say that the experience of getting together every evening in an attitude of prayer, kneeling on the large carpet of my mother's room, instilled in me the "good habit" of recollecting myself before going to bed. This habit remained, and it gradually became something I desired, something full of meaning.

I think the important thing is that we parents keep in mind what is essential in prayer. This is what a mother told me: "I realized that when I put the children to bed and said the Our Father and Hail Mary with them, I felt a sense of relief, as if to say, 'They said their prayers this evening too. They're in good shape." Actually they hadn't done anything. Out of laziness I did more or less the external part, but I didn't help the children find a true — even if very brief — relationship with God. It required a little time, some moments of calm, a short preliminary conversation about the day just finished. It required, in other words, a little more love on my part. Then it became natural to say thank you for something, to ask forgiveness, to make a suggestion . . . ."

"There are children that are very active and a little rebellious," as another mother put it, "who find it very hard to say prayers. I understood soon enough that my second child, four years old, did not want to say his prayers. He didn't even want to make the sign of the cross. I tried to convince him with sweet talk. A few times I insisted. But I felt I couldn't go on this way. At last I decided. For many days I didn't make him say prayers at all. During the day, however, I told him some short but interesting story taken from Scripture, especially from the Gospels. One evening as was putting on his pajamas, he asked me, 'What about our prayers?' So without showing any surprise I had him say a short prayer made up right there on the spot."

What I think should be absolutely avoided are the cute little rhymes, perhaps said in baby talk. They're certainly not prayer. Also, always praying to baby Jesus, on the assumption that he is more available to the little ones, is a mistake. It distorts the idea of God in the child. The child too is made to know God, and he has the innate capacity to know Him.

Another mistaken approach to the relationship with God through prayer is that of bothering the children with that constant "You have to pray. Did you do what you were told? Did you say your prayers?" This attitude creates in the little ones a subservient mentality in relation to God, Prayer becomes something that God demands, something that must be paid to God as a tribute. Unfortunately children acquire this kind of mentality very easily.

A mother reported to me that very often, when going to bed in the evening, her child would say, "I'm tired this evening. I'll just make the sign of the cross." or "I'm really sleepy. Will Jesus mind if I only say a Hail Mary?" For a while she didn't do anything about it. Finally, one evening she decided to confront the problem head on. "Listen here," she said to him. "Why do you always go through this routine? Do you by chance think that the Lord needs those few words that we say to him — and say so poorly? To tell you the truth, I don't think God knows quite what to do with those broken records that we keep playing for him. It's we, instead, who need him. What we have to do is spend some moments with him, talk to him, tell him about our affairs, tell him that we love him, and ask him to continue to love us, to help us to be better; we have to thank him for all he gives us, don't you think? Sure, we're lazy and distracted by many things, and prayer is hard for us. But we have to remember that the Lord does not need contact with us, even though he wants it because he loves us. On the other hand, we aren't worth anything without contact with him."

## Religious Articles

One day while I was looking at a copy of the 16th-century painting of the Madonna that was hanging in a bedroom, I asked myself, "What will go through Michael's head when he looks at that picture?" He was three at the time. I felt I understood then that the religious items we adults like and sometimes consider conducive to prayerfulness, quite often do nothing for children, even if they are works of art. I don't mean by this that children don't need religious articles. But they have to be beautiful, simple, and right for their age. A madonna with child won't bother them. Of course they don't understand it at once. At first they'll think it's just a mother, with a child like them. The face of a smiling angel on the cradle will perhaps convey a sense of serenity and protectiveness.

I think, however, that pictures and images will have a negative and harmful effect on their future faith if we show an "attachment" to them. If, for example, we always pray before a certain painting, they might connect prayer with that particular image.

A father said to me, "I've always been careful not to present to my young children that popular picture of God the Father that depicts him as a grand old man with a beard. As adults the children will have a hard time shedding this image, and their manner of thinking about God will remain limited. I think it's much better not to delineate an idea of God with specific features and contours that limit children's thoughts of him and suffocate their spiritual intuitions."

I can only agree with such a wise and well-founded opinion. It's good to give the child — as much as possible — the opportunity to intuit according to his own capacities the mystery of a transcendent God.

But it will be said that if we don't show the child images of God, he won't be able to conceive of God as a person. He'll have a vague idea of him. He'll have some difficulty believing in the existence of a reality that doesn't appear to his senses. This isn't mistaken. Still, for the child, the fact that his parents, in whom he has the greatest trust and who would never deceive him, speak with someone is often sufficient reason for him to understand that they are speaking to a true and living person. I have often heard children under four years of age say, "You can't see God, but he's there." While, on the other hand, they've never said to me, "I can't see him, so he's not there." This perhaps would be said by children who have lived in a materialistic, pagan environment.

I believe that the child needs images, especially when he begins to get a little older. In speaking of Moses and of Jacob, in recounting things from the life of Jesus, it's important to illustrate what we say and to fix it in their minds through the aid of images and figures.

"I was very little," my husband said, "when my godmother gave me a book on the birth of Jesus. I still remember perfectly all the pages of that book, the colors, the atmosphere I entered when I opened it and began to page through it. Of course I didn't know how to read yet. I read the pictures. And I recall other illustrated books on sacred history that were popular at that time. I can still see Moses, Gideon, and many other great figures."

These are impressions that last for the rest of one's life.

And when children are intently interested in a certain part of a book, they examine the pictures very carefully. They want to find all those elements that impressed them in the story.

In our house, we had a print by Fra Angelico of the flight into Egypt. I had already told Francis, then four years old, of this episode in the life of Jesus. He was drawing one day, and I noticed that every so often he would look up at the print. All of a sudden he came close to it and studied it intently. Then with a smile of relief he said to me, "I knew that St. Joseph couldn't be angry. He's just serious and worried because they have to make a long trip!"

The difficulty for us parents, then, is to choose prints, books, and pictures that are beautiful, vibrant, expressive, rich in detail. And to tell the truth, often we can't find these things in stores. Those you see are often overly sentimental; they're too pious and unreal. However, by uniting ourselves with the simplicity of children, we should be able to find something more suited to them than to our adult tastes.

In any case, it seems more necessary than ever that parents be guided in this area by their common sense and their sensitivity. Only they have the instinctive intuition for what their children most need. What I want to emphasize is that the children, no matter what age they are, should always be helped to go beyond what is physical in order to grasp what is transcendent. Images are means for approaching God and drawing near to him. They should not become ends in themselves, and obscure the things of God.

## Liturgical Feasts

To give the reality of the faith to my children and to deepen it in them, I have, from their earliest childhood, taken advantage of the feast days in the liturgical year. In this way, religious education and instruction can come about in a very normal manner and coincide with a participation in the life of others — of families that they know and of the world that surrounds them.

At Christmas, for example, it's normal for them to ask something about the birth of Jesus. I tell them about it perhaps while going to gather some straw for the crib, for the construction of the crib is a yearly event. Of course there are the folkloristic aspects and the novelty; there are many elements that cooperate to make it a charming activity. But the atmosphere of Christmas Eve, when we put baby Jesus in the manger; the short but fervent prayer by the light of a candle; and also their work on the crib in the following days (the little figures are never in the same place;

Mary and Joseph are moving all over the stable) — these certainly leave some impression on their minds and their hearts.

Similarly, Easter and Pentecost and the feast days of Mary can provide the opportunity for stories and conversations. Naturally this is always to be done with discretion, taking account of their needs and their maturity, as well as their desire to listen and know.

Through the liturgical year, our everyday life and that two-thousand-year-old reality converge. And it can be the beginning of their participation in the liturgy of the Church.

My experiences are confirmed by other mothers. Here's what one says. "One Christmas when my little girl was two, she asked me, 'Mommy, what is Christmas?' She probably heard this strange world mentioned many times. It's the birth of Jesus!' I answered. 'Jesus is the son of God. God sent us his son, Jesus, because he loves us. He loves us by sending his son and by sending also all the children in the various families of the world. Jesus and all children are the fruit of love.' By telling her this as a starting point, I then could tell her more things about God and our relationship with him. 'Since God is the source of Love, every time we are loving our daddies or mommies or brothers or other people, we are doing something that is the Love of God. We become like him, and in this relationship, in this love, we find our only happiness.' Thinking it over again, it's hard to believe that she could understand this conversation. Yet I recall that she understood very well, and I realized afterwards that she has been deeply impressed by it."

## Taking the Little Ones to Church

"What is the best age to begin taking the children to Church?" many mothers and fathers often ask. The question is a good one, and keeping it in mind in the course of our interviews, we asked many parents what they thought. Well, judging by what many of them have told us, we can conclude that there is no set age. It depends on many things. It depends on the type of child, on his maturity and sensitivities, and also on the fact that certain situations force parents at times to bring their children to church if they want to go themselves.

But let's consider the child first. His initial impressions are very important. As for me, I brought my children to church very early, trying however to avoid bringing them when the church was too crowded or when there were moments of confusion. They liked church. Maybe they liked the largeness of it, or those shiny floors that invited them to do some sliding. Maybe they liked the lights or the candles. Who knows? Perhaps later on they were attracted by the air of mysteriousness and silence.

In general, when they were little, I didn't say anything to them. I tried, as much as possible to allow them movement, to let them look around. To a certain extent, I didn't pay attention to them. Later when they began to know Jesus, I said, pointing to the tabernacle, "There's Jesus," and that's all. Still later we began to say hello to him together and recite some short prayers. For a long time, they kept the habit of saying "Hello Jesus" when entering or passing a church.

But what about those very lively and restless children who can't stay still a minute in church? It's definitely better not to bring them when they're small. Normally, though, our children are pleased to come with us, just as long as we don't keep them there too long. They like to do what adults do. One of my children at three or four years of age always went into the confessional, quite pleased at doing what his mommy did.

One day, Frank was about five, he was sitting in the pew with what seemed to me a look of distraction. I turned to him and said, "Say a Hail Mary." He gave me a look of disappointment, and I realized at once that I had disturbed him. Certainly he wasn't praying the way I would expect him to, but maybe he was experiencing the atmosphere of the church far more than I. How do we know what's really going on inside them?

On another occasion, I noticed him pull a toy car out of his pocket and begin to play with it, rolling it up and down the pew. So I scolded him and told him to sit still, and I added, "Don't you love Jesus?" "Sure I love Jesus, but I can't just sit and do nothing but think of him all the time. Why can I play at home and not in church? Jesus sees me at home too!" What a lesson he gave me! I tried, however, to tell him gently that playing in church disturbs other persons who "come to stay a while with Jesus."

## The Mass

Having had five children, we've often found ourselves going to Sunday Mass with children of different ages. One Sunday, at noon Mass, I noticed Frank was exasperated. "Don't you understand what the priest is saying?" I asked. "I don't *want* to listen because I don't like it," he answered with a decisive tone of voice. I was annoyed by the agressiveness of his answer, but happy too because of his sincerity. I made an examination of conscience.

Actually we often drag our children into participation in liturgical functions that are not adapted to them. It's not unusual, that is, for us to bring them because it's more convenient for us. It might be more difficult, for example, to get up earlier and take them to the children's Mass; or maybe we want to drive somewhere and end up bringing them, dead tired to evening Mass. Perhaps we drag them along against their will because we haven't made an effort to find someone to watch them during that hour. Then we expect them to be still and attentive. Attentive to what, if they don't understand anything?

One mother was worried about the hostility her little boy had toward the Mass. "He was very interested in stories from Scripture, in talks about spiritual things. He tried in his little way to have an evangelical attitude toward his sister. But even if he want to church willingly, the Mass was too long for him, and he understood nothing. Thus, the few times that he had come with us, because we didn't have anyone to leave him with, he made it clear that he had come only as a favor to me, and that he was bored. It was like this when he was five, five and a half, six, six and a half. We were always at the same point. In fact, it had become worse. He objected, 'I'm not at the age when I have to go, so there's nothing wrong if I don't go to Mass!' However, I saw the age of obligatory attendance approaching, and there was no improvement. Fortunately, at that time our parish was gathering the children together on Saturday afternoon. My husband and I decided to send him, and since he always liked being with other children, he went very willingly. After playing for a while, they listened to a short talk, at the end of which the priest said: 'So then, we'll meet tomorrow at ten o'clock Mass.' When he came home, he said to us, 'Tomorrow there's a Mass for me at ten. Are we going?' From that day on, he went regularly to Mass on Sunday. I think it's understandable. The ten o'clock Mass is adapted to them. The sermon is brief and within their grasp. Above all, he finds himself praying with other children like him. To tell the truth, we never thought that a Mass like that was necessary for him."

At times it's enough for parents to find the time and the way of explaining the meaning of the service they are attending. This is what a father said: "One day, just before he was to receive Communion, I told my son what Mass was like in the times of the early Christians, shortly after the death of Jesus. I told him how the people met in each other's homes, ate a meal (perhaps sharing what they brought with them), spoke together and told one another things about their lives. In other words, they loved one another so well that they were all just like members of the same family. And then they all received Jesus. 'In our times,' I explained, 'Christians are so numerous that we can't do this in our homes with a few persons that we know and love! So maybe it's not as beautiful, and perhaps it bores you to be in church among all those people you don't know. Let's hope that, little by little, we all love one another better. But in the meantime be patient. In our Mass there is the same living and true Jesus.' "

Here's what two other parents say: "For a while we were going every Sunday with our children to a Mass in which about one hundred people, including families that we knew intimately, participated. In addition, the children knew the priest. The Mass had well-prepared songs and prayers, and everyone participated very fully. You could feel the community. My smallest son was two then, and the other children not much older. Yet they were happy to be there, or better, to take part. They sang and responded; and they themselves asked us to bring them there."

### The Sacraments

The child always begins to perceive the value of the sacraments through the example of his parents.

The mother of three lively boys told me this. "From their infancy the children saw me and my husband going to Mass every morning, first one of us, then the other, in order not to leave them home alone. As time passed, the two older ones began to come too, while the smallest one stayed at home with one of us. One day, he too said he wanted to come to church, and from that time on, we all went together. Of course the smallest one was a little restless. He found it hard to remain still for more than two minutes. I began to ask myself if it wouldn't be better for him to stay at home. One day I shared my perplexity with the other two. 'Don't you think it would be better if we left Paul at home? How can Jesus be happy with the way he disturbs everyone?' The oldest said, 'Maybe Jesus is happier with him than with all the others who go to church. How can you tell?' He taught me a lesson. Well, one day, Paul was becoming obsessed with an unrestrainable desire to go to confession! From that time on, whenever I went to confession, my husband had to hold him down, and when he went, I had to do the same. But it was a frantic situation. He wouldn't listen to reason. He was only five, but he wanted to confess too. This went on until one day a priest who had watched this scene more than once said to me, 'Well let him come!' A bit taken by surprise, I asked Paul carefully before letting him go, 'Now that you can go to confession, what do you intend to say to Fr. Tom?' We had never spoken about confession to him; none of us had explained what its purpose was. 'I'll tell him that I always disobey you!' he answered. He had understood that in going there and getting down on his knees, he had to have something to accuse himself of, and he had no doubts about what it was!"

Another mother said this: "The period preceding the first Communion of my oldest child was very beautiful and profound for all of us. My husband and I were especially aware of the responsibility the period of preparation placed on us. First of all we felt it was necessary to make an effort to live better, with more depth and greater love between us and with the children. We felt the need to maintain an atmosphere of harmony in the house — an atmosphere created by little acts of attention, of sensitivity, of mercy. I remember how one evening we gathered together with all the children and we renewed our Baptismal promises. From that moment on, every member of the family grew in charity; this was, I think, the special characteristic of that period. I remember how we made the house especially tidy, and bought some beautiful white flowers for his first confession. We wanted the external part of the occasion to be especially cheerful too, so that it would highlight the subtle beauty of that moment."

And here is one more testimony. "My daughter is five years old. She hasn't yet made her first Communion. She's observed, however, that my husband and I receive the Eucharist frequently and perhaps she's heard us talk between ourselves about this sacrament. Or perhaps she was impressed by the sermons. The fact is that one day she asked me, 'Why can't I receive Holy Communion?' 'Because,' I answered, 'the Church has established that a child should not receive Communion before the age of seven or eight, so that he will be able to understand what it means to receive Jesus,' 'I'm five years old and I know very well what receiving Jesus means,' she responded. 'It means to eat him so he can grow in us so that we will be able to become him. There! Now I can receive Communion. Maybe I can't say my thanksgiving, but if I receive Communion with you and you say your thanksgiving out loud instead of to yourself the way you usually do, I can say it along with you. Then I can learn to say the thanksgiving prayer like everyone else. So I don't see why I have to wait till I'm seven before making my first Communion.' "

## Don't Push Them

We've discussed introducing prayer, the sacraments, and liturgy to the child and we've seen that experiences are personal and different. The point I would like to insist upon is that, whatever our method and attitude may be, we always have to be careful not to push, not to control rigidly the free expression of our children's interior life, for it comes to the surface and develops slowly. Here are some experiences that show this, I think.

"Both my children have made their first Communion. It was a deepening of their relationship with God for them — a lasting experience, not momentary and transitory. This may have been the result of our preparation. Every chance I had, I tried to help them see the effects that daily Communion had on my interior life and my external behavior. Little by little they could feel the link between the Eucharist and my behavior. Yet, now they don't feel the need to go to Communion every day. They go willingly to Sunday Mass and of course receive Communion. I'd say that, for them, it doesn't make sense to attend Mass and not receive Jesus. As for Mass and Communion during the week, this happens only in special cases, such as a birthday or a special anniversary, when it seems fairly normal to go. Otherwise they don't feel the need. Every time I tried to suggest they join me, the invitation was not accepted, so I never insisted.

"Once Holy Thursday we were planning to go to Mass. It was cold and raining. Because the second oldest of my nine children had no intention of coming

(She was in a period of strong rebellion), I asked her to stay at home with the smallest one. As I started to leave with the others, my son Mark, seeing that his older sister remained at home, or perhaps wanting to avoid the inclement weather, said, "You know, I almost feel like staying at home myself!" I didn't like this, especially because I felt it was a negative reflection of his sister's negative attitude. but I said nothing and left him at home. Later, about half way through the Mass, into the Church he came, all wet and muddy. But after he joined us, he noticed that one of his little sisters wasn't there — Regina, who had wanted to come to Mass but stopped off on the way to get a friend. Perhaps she forgot to come and didn't notice that the time had passed. Well, Mark ran out of church and returned five minutes later, even wetter than before, but holding the hand of his little sister.

"It was Wednesday of Holy Week and we were preparing to go away to spend Easter with relatives. I had left my son at the barber shop and I had then gone to my usual hairdresser. We agreed to meet at twelve in front of the Cathedral.

"As I was crossing the street, I saw he was already waiting at the church door. 'I'm going to Mass,' I said. 'It's starting right now. If you want to come too, you'll be able to go to confession for Easter,' 'Nah!' he said, 'I don't feel like it. I'd rather go to confession in Grandpa's parish.' 'Okay,' I said, a little opposed but not showing my feelings. 'Take a walk around here for half an hour. Daddy will pass by here at 12:45 to pick us up and we'll go.' I smiled at him and then entered the church. While I was trying to recollect myself, I was assailed by the doubts that I had overcome a thousand times before, but which nevertheless kept popping up. 'Did I do the right thing? Sure, it's important to leave him free, but don't parents have an obligation to direct their children, to prod them on, especially when they're young?' In the end, I came to my usual conclusion: 'Lord, if I made a mistake, please correct it; you handle the situation.'

"Holy Thursday and Good Friday I went to the services in my father's parish. All the children my son's age, who had played with him during the day, were altar boys at the services. But after they left him in the yard, he went straight into the house and sat down to watch T.V.

"On Saturday, he asked me unexpectedly, "What time are you going to church this evening?' 'There's no Mass this evening. The priest isn't celebrating midnight Mass this year. All there is, is the recitation of the penitential Psalms and confession from seven to eight.' 'This evening, I'm going,' he said resolutely. I said nothing.

"Just a little before eight, a T.V. program my son liked very much began, yet he hurried to his room, combed his hair, and changed his clothes. A few minutes later, he skipped down the stairs and said, 'See you later, I'm going to church!' and he left. When he came back, we were sitting at the table. His face was radiant and his eyes sparkling. 'I bought something good for everybody at the store.' He took out a little candy bag and poured out no less than a pound of fruit candies bought with the change he had in his pocket. Later, just before we were going to bed, we were alone together. 'Mom,' he burst out, 'everything's different. I'm really happy. I've gotten back in touch with Jesus. You know, it's been a long time that I've been away from Him. Even when I went to confession before, I tried to fool myself by saying, "This isn't sin, that's not important . . ." I like to say the bad words that some of my friends say, and then I tried to convince myself that it wasn't a big thing. I argued, I hit my friends, and then I told myself that I was in the right. Now I've made a real good confession: I told everything, and I feel so good!'

"You see, then, for him it was an important experience. For he made a deeply personal examination of conscience. Would the confession of the previous Wednesday have had the same effect? I really don't think so.

"I had gone to Mass during the week in a little chapel of a religious order of priests I know. Because there was a playground nearby, I brought my little boy so he could play outside a little. While I was in church, a priest of the community whom we know very well saw him playing. 'Hi. What are you doing?' 'Playing.' 'Where's your Mommy?' 'At Mass.' 'How come you didn't go with her?' 'I didn't want to. I'd rather play outside.' 'What did your mother say about that?' 'Nothing.' And he continued playing. 'But,' the priest prodded on, 'if you don't feel like going to Mass on Sunday, doesn't your Mommy say anything either?' 'What do you mean?!' the boy exclaimed with an air of indignation. 'On Sunday, I *do* feel like going to Mass.'"

## Forming the Conscience

If we truly want to educate our children and thereby get them used to standing on their own feet, able to tell good from evil, to distinguish what God wants from what he doesn't want, and to freely choose what way they should follow, it is necessary to help them form their consciences. When they face life, and have to translate their principles into behavior, a sensitive, well-formed conscience will be their starting point, their foundation.

I asked many mothers how they have tried to carry out this duty. "Mainly, it's *my* conscience that is formed through contact with them," one mother told me. "For example, when I'm lacking in charity, I realize it immediately from the way they look at me. Because, if a remark of a scolding is given with love, they accept and understand it. When it is done in anger — not for their good but for my satisfaction, my advantage — they reject it. I think that my desire to form their conscience becomes an effort to develop my own. I think that theirs is to be built upon mine, upon ours. Therefore, I have to behave in a way consistent with my beliefs, if I am to make them consistent. I can't expect to form their conscience if I don't form my own."

To help the children have consciences that are more sensitive and refined, and to deepen our relationship with them, we can try making an examination of conscience with them. Not in a rigid manner, of course, but with simplicity. It should be a confidential and relaxed dialogue in which parents and children review the day that has gone by. The children will get great joy from it and often great comfort. When they are able to open up, or even to point out something about another, with trust in the love and mercy of their parents and of God, they are free from many burdens. Nothing will lodge in their souls, so to speak, weighing them down and making them ill at ease.

Naturally, formation of conscience is principally aimed at making us avoid evil, error, what is commonly called sin. But within the picture that we've been drawing, in which everything is rooted in a trust in God-Love, sin (like everything else) takes on a new perspective.

To show what I mean, I'll include the experiences of two mothers. "This bugaboo of sin weighed more than a little on my infancy and youth," one said. "It prevented me from setting my relationship with God straight. I wasn't able to have a true love and trust in God; I could not give myself totally to him. This being did not inspire much confidence in me, because I felt that if I did something to enjoy life or avoid too much boredom, it offended him and he would plan some more punishment for me. Then I understood — I should say, I discovered — that God is Love, and that if we wanted to resemble him even slightly, we had to make a continuous effort to love. My narrow view of sin disappeared. I learned that the one way to avoid sin was to try never to stop loving. What freedom this brought! I tried to give this understanding of sin to my son. I explained that what is bad is simply not an expression of love that is within us. When he went to his first Confession, he returned home all radiant. 'Isn't it wonderful!' he said to me. 'I've freed myself of all my failures to love. Now I'm ready to love everybody, always.' "

And another mother: "When my child had to go to confession for the first time, he came to me, worried. 'Mommy, what's sin?' he asked. 'I don't know what to say to the priest.' 'Look,' I answered, 'I think that sin is a lack of love. Let's see now. Disobedience is a lack of love toward your Mommy or Daddy. Not studying well, not showing respect for your teacher, annoying your brother and sister, arguing with a friend — these things are all a lack of love toward all these persons.' He understood quite well. His confessions (I know it because often we would prepare for them together) are now totally based on love. For example, 'I didn't see Jesus in my mommy, and I disobeyed her; I could have made my little brother happy by letting him use my soldiers, but I didn't do it and he cried.' This perspective helps him to grasp little by little, as he grows up, the true essence of sin (which is the lack of love); and it forces him to interact intensely with others. It increases the need to love in him, and this carries him far beyond the simple avoidance of sin."

Another mother highlighted the importance of giving children a sense of responsibility.

"A most important and delicate job for those responsible for educating a child is to help him form his conscience in the right way. I've seen more than once that the conscience begins to form very early in children. One must be careful that the child becomes neither superficial nor scrupulous. When his conscience then begins to 'function,' so to speak, I have found that it's a very good thing to allow it to do its work. Every time I left my child free to follow his conscience rather than one of my orders — after explaining the circumstances to him and indicating what should be done — he did it more willingly. And I saw that he took a step forward in the growth of his personality.

"Often children tend instinctively to assert their personalities by putting up resistance against established authority. Moreover, children (like most of us) have a good dose of laziness that makes them drag out and argue about what they have to do. I remember one time, when I had told my son to do something, he answered, 'No.' to me, and gave me some sort of excuse. 'Do as you please,' I said as agreeably as I could, in order to cut things short. 'You're free. But look inside yourself first and then decide.' 'Oh Mommy!' was his reaction. 'When you say it like that I feel inside that I have to do it!' 'Yes, I know,' I thought to myself, somewhat pleased, 'With *me* you can argue; you can convince *me* it's better to do differently. But with your conscience, there's no escape!.'"

Because I think its clear and useful, I'd also like to cite an experience of a mother who has a background in psychology.

"Despite some opinions, I think that a Christian education avoids the formation of complexes, especially the guilt complex. This is true, even if a child has — as mine does — a conscience so sensitive that he has a tendency to become scrupulous. I think this complex is easily overcome by children who have learned to trust in the love of God, and who have the attitude of always living 'the present moment,' entrusting the past to the mercy of Jesus. Here is in episode to illustrate this.

"One evening Luke was very restless and naughty when he was eating, and he made my husband and me very nervous. After supper, I put him to bed earlier than usual to help him understand that what he did was wrong. For a while he was very sulky and quiet. Then, all at once, almost in tears, he burst out, 'I was really bad, really bad. I really was a bad boy!' And he wouldn't calm down. So I put it to him this way: "You're right, but Jesus forgives a lot of things because of an act of love. Now, if you begin at once to love Jesus without thinking any longer about what has happened, if, for instance, you get undressed quickly and hang up your clothes for Jesus, what you did at the table will be erased completely. Otherwise, if you keep thinking about what you did wrong before, you'll do what you're doing now poorly.'

"Obviously delighted with this solution, he undressed himself quickly, recited his prayers solemnly, and jumped under the covers, exclaiming, 'Mommy, I'm happy!' So now, if he does something that's not right, he doesn't let his soul get weighed down. He comes to tell me everything. He's learned to appreciate the joy of entrusting his little faults to the love of Jesus — and of his mother. In particular, before going to sleep he developed the habit of telling me all his faults, and he doesn't feel at ease unless he does so. On the basis of this experience, I am convinced that this kind of examination of conscience, begun so spontaneously and with such simplicity, not only keeps his soul peaceful but helps him develop a more refined conscience.

chapter four

**The Religious Perspective
of Daily Events:
The Meaning of Suffering**

## Radical Questions

In our lives at home with our children, we try to give a Christian impetus to their behavior and to our own. The real test of our faith, and of theirs, is the way we handle the situations and circumstances and events of each day. And we find that the most serious problems we have to solve are those of injustice, poverty, discrimination, misfortune, sickness, death — in general, problems of suffering.

"God is love. How can he allow all this? The one who really believes in the love of God and has experienced it, finds the answer for himself, and also for his children. In fact, whether we can grasp the true meaning of any particular suffering or not, will depend almost totally on our having a coherent way of looking at things in terms of God's love. The children, however, will grasp the real truth of religion by seeing how their parents can remain calm and full of trust when they face suffering. And they will also see how practical this religious view is since with this strength they can face any difficulty whatever. Soon they too will be able to have this experience: that following God and believing in his love truly results in a richness beyond measure, in a peace and joy that is worth going after even when the road gets steep.

## Poverty and Providence

"Dad, there's something I don't understand," Frank said to my husband one day. "God created the first trees and vegetables. He created the sun and the water to make them grow. He created the sheep and the cows, the chickens and the rabbits, and all the rest. And he gave it all to us as a gift so we could eat. It was a *gift*, right?" "Sure!" my husband answered, not knowing what my son was leading up to. "Well then, why do we have to buy things now, and what about those who don't have the money — why don't they get anything?" I listened closely to find out how my husband would handle these questions. After explaining in very simple words the ideas how the use of money and private property came about, he calmly told our son that this very strange and sick situation that he had grasped with the logic of a child was caused by human selfishness. Men often tend to be greedy, to take more than is necessary for themselves and to leave the weaker ones, the less shrewd, and often the best people empty-handed. "Look," he concluded, "If people had lived the mutual love that Jesus told us to have before he died, everyone would possess what is necessary, and even more. If we try to love one another, if love among men — and especially among Christians — increases, all the differences and the injustices will vanish. This is because Providence, the love of God for humanity, has given us all we need, and all we have to do is divide it up well, as brothers."

A young mother told me of having spoken in this way to her children.

"In our home, the children have always heard from me or from my husband that Providence is the love with which God cares for us and gives us all we need to feed ourselves, to dress ourselves, in other words, to live. However, we've also always stressed this point: We keep what we need, what is indispensable; but we give to others what isn't necessary. If we fail to do this, there will always be inequities. We've done things this way so that the children, though they are still small, would feel the great problems of the world, would know that poverty and hunger exist, that children are dying.... For them too, the question of why there is Providence for some and not for others comes up. 'God,' we've often explained, 'is Love and is Providence for everybody. However, he wants us also to be love and providence for others. And so, if we don't allow material goods to circulate among us, Providence comes to a halt, not only for others, but also for us.'

"Well, this is what happened one year at Easter. My children had received a large chocolate egg from a friend. It was the only one they had received that Easter. We were preparing to leave to spend Easter with their grandmother, and we decided to ask the children if they wouldn't mind giving that egg to the child of a family of modest means that we knew, so we wouldn't have to carry it along on the trip. We didn't have to ask twice. They took it to the boy themselves, and they were cheerful and happy. When we arrived at Grandmother's, they found uncles and aunts and relatives from all over, and all of them had brought chocolate eggs for the children. So, on Easter day, there were fifteen eggs of the most varied sizes in the house. 'You see that, Uncle?' my oldest daughter said to my brother. 'It's really true that Providence exists. Before coming here, we had only one chocolate egg, and we gave it to our friend Peter. Now we've come here, and Jesus has given us fifteen in exchange for one.' "

On the other hand, the fact that God allows some of his sons to be in want (the very God who said, "Do not worry about what you will eat, about what you are to put on ... look at the birds of the air, the lillies of the fields") can be seen in a positive light. Poverty, if accepted as a means of purification and sanctification, can be very fruitful. This is illustrated by the following account, which a woman gave me.

"There was a period in which our family was in a really bad economic situation. Then, unexpectedly, my husband lost his job. For the first months, we took care of the necessities with the little money we had saved (very little, because with children you can't save too much). Then things got really bad. Yet we never lost trust in God and in his help. We tried to renew our faith and believe that God loved us even in this trial. I don't recall ever having felt so strongly that only God counts, that he is the only true wealth. It often helped me to read that passage of the Gospel that says, 'look for the kingdom of God and his justice, and the rest will be given to you in abundance.' I always repeated it to the children too, together with the beatitudes described by Jesus in his Sermon on the Mount: 'Blessed are the poor in spirit ... Blessed are those who weep ... Blessed are those who hunger and thirst for justice . . .' This experience served also to make us realize how many things we were attached to, how many things had become our god. Then, friends came to our aid with their love and concern. Finally, my husband was offered a good job and we got back on our feet again."

This element of detachment, of poverty of spirit, of the choice of God before all else, seems to me to be authentic Christianity. And Jesus promised the "hundredfold" and eternal life to those who leave everything for him. It's a very good practice to try to convey these principles to children as they begin their Christian lives. Moreover, they show themselves more disposed than we are to put what they have understood into practice, as the following episode shows.

"Just before Christmas, in fact, on the last day of school before the Christmas holidays, I went with Luke to the school where my husband taught. The priest who was principal had had a large tree put up, and underneath it he had put gifts for each of the students. Luke was expecting one too, but the principal did not know he would be there and so there was none for him. Little by little, as Fr. John called the boys up and the gifts became fewer, my son became more and more silent. Finally he rushed out of the hall crying and saying between his sobs, 'There's nothing for me!' I had warned him this might happen and he promised that he wouldn't expect anything. I repeated to him what I had said, but with an effort to suffer with him in this little sorrow of his. After a few minutes, as we were leaving, he started to smile and said, 'I know it. I came here to love, but

I guess I forgot that I should expect nothing in return.' We sat down on a bench. At that moment, a father of one of the students was walking by and, seeing us, said, 'Luke! You're here! Wait a minute while I go back to the car to get a present I have for you.' In that same moment, a boy came running out saying, 'Luke, Luke, Fr. John is looking for you! Come quickly! Thre's a present for you.' With these words, Luke got up, his face aglow, and said to me. 'I feel happy. Maybe I've become detached . . . . I've got the hundred-fold!' "

## The Corrective Value of Suffering

Children don't find it hard to understand that sufferings — even small sufferings, like inconveniences, disappointments, and tiny sacrifices — can have a corrective function. They have a daily experience of this in the family when their mothers and fathers correct them, maybe a little harshly sometimes, for their good, so that they can become better.

This is what a father told me: "I've seen that my children are convinced that God is a father who watches out for us to the point that if bringing us back to what is good requires even a few 'smacks,' he'll do it. He permits us to suffer a little since this is exactly what we usually need to straighten us out, to help us begin loving again." And a friend of mine said, "How often when I was little I heard mothers say to their children, 'Don't do that or God will punish you.' 'Don't do that or you'll make Jesus cry.' Or when their children didn't take their advice and got into trouble because of it, they would say, 'Do you see how Jesus is punishing you?' I didn't know why, but every time I heard such things, I got the shivers; it was like hearing a knife scratch across a plate or chalk on a blackboard! Instinctively I understood that this wasn't the right angle to take."

When it came time for me to begin educating my own son, I naturally tried to avoid these errors. Soon I discovered that my son often disobeyed me and did something wrong because of stubborness or egoism. But I always tried to repeat to him, "God loves us all, and you know that when someone loves, he wants the happiness of the person he loves. God wants us to be good because he knows that this is the only way we'll be happy." "It's true," he would say, "When I'm good, when I give away something I like or I obey you, then afterwards I'm happy." "Right. Now it often happens that we forget this, and in one way or another God reminds us of it; he rings some sort of alarm to tell us that we're on the wrong track."

This reminds me of something that happened a few years ago when Luke was very small and we lived in an apartment. He received a mechanical toy, something like a pinball machine, that shot a spinning metal ball along a track at various heights, depending on the ability of the player. We were about to go out on some errands, and Luke wanted to bring along this toy. I explained to him that it didn't seem the best thing to do, but he didn't want to listen to reason. With an air of defiance, he got into the elevator, gripping the toy with both hands. On the ground floor, as he was getting out, the metal ball slipped from his hand and fell right into the crack between the elevator and the shift. It was irretrievable. Luke stood there for a moment with a look of confusion and surprise. Then he said, "Jesus really loves me. He doesn't let me get away with anything. He rings the alarm!' "

## The Coredemptive Value of Suffering

For Christians, suffering and the cross have a coredemptive function. When a child realizes that Jesus loved us so much as to suffer and die for us, he doesn't find it hard to accept the idea that his personal suffering too can be transformed into love for others and thereby take on very great value.

"My six-year-old had to undergo an operation on her eye," a young mother told me. "We were in the hospital for fifteen days and the whole thing was very hard for her. The first week she had to have many tests — blood tests and other such things that bothered her very much. 'I don't mind the hospital,' she confided to me, 'It's like a hotel. But when they give me shots, when they take blood from me . . . . I don't like that.' Then one day she said, 'Why is Jesus asking me to have an operation on my eye?' It was a logical question for her. She had learned to believe in the love of Jesus for her. 'I can't tell you why he's asked you to have an operation on your eyes,' I answered her. 'But one thing I can tell you. Because God loves us, he sent his Son down to earth to save us. However, because he could count on him, he asked a great deal of his Son. He asked everything. He asked even his life. If we are really other sons of God and brothers of Jesus, we must try to have the same feeling in our souls that Jesus had towards his father. We have to be ready to give God all that he asks. So that if today he is asking an operation on your eye of you, it means that he can count on you. Who knows what he will do with this operation? Great things, things we may never know about. Maybe because of this operation, he will be able to feed who knows how many hungry children. Or maybe he will give a distressed father the strength to carry his family ahead. Or maybe he'll bring happiness to someone who's unhappy, in prison perhaps. Maybe he could find a way to reconcile two enemies. Why your operation? I can't answer that. I only know that the more God asks, the more he trusts in that child of whom he is asking something.'

"These words of mine were enough to keep her calm and serene throughout her hospital stay. I was surprised how much she understood from this, since I didn't talk about the Mystical Body, as perhaps I would have with an adult. A short while after, when my child had already come out of the hospital, something happened.

"She went one day to visit the mother of a friend of ours. This woman had been paralyzed for thirty years with a crippling arthritis. She sat in a chair with her hands all contracted, almost rigid. But she was a person I wouldn't hesitate to call a saint, because of the patience with which she supported this torment. She was always easy-going, gracious, pleasant, never turned in on herself, interested in everybody. I was worried that on seeing her, my daughter would be a little upset or that she might unknowingly say something inappropriate. Since she went with some friends, they could tell me later that she had been very affectionate and kind, and that looking at the woman, she had comforted her with childlike simplicity. She had said, 'Aunty, Jesus must count on you very much because my Mommy told me that when Jesus trusts a person a lot, he asks a lot of that person. And Jesus is asking a lot from you.' "

And here is how a father explained how inconvenience, tiredness, and suffering have value as offerings. "It often happens that my son gets annoyed or bored for just any reason. For example, on a long trip he might grumble. At such times I might say, 'What good is it to grumble? You'll be bored whether you do or you don't. Let's offer the annoyance to Jesus, who told us to come to him when we are carrying a burden (Matt. 11.28), so that he can make use of it in any way he likes. Let's do it together. What do you say?' He often likes the idea and his boredom disappears. I've also asked him if he feels closer to Jesus when he prays or when he makes this little offering. 'When I make this offering,' he's answered me. Thus, in our house we have these little efforts at kindness, generosity, obedience, and so forth, but we try to make them all end up as offerings. And the idea of an offering, since it is a positive and free act, is not displeasing to my son or to his little sisters. In fact, their habit of prayer stemmed from this, for true prayer is made possible by such free offerings. Otherwise prayers can become useless nursery rhymes, quite superficial. There is the danger that prayer will fall into the same category as brushing our teeth or putting on our pajamas."

## Death

Children are faced with the question of death very early. This happens despite the many different methods that are used to avoid telling them about it by adults who themselves haven't resolved the question. Sometimes adults invent "pious" lies to hide the loss of some loved one. They fail to realize that this topic is very important in the religious education of their children because it also involves their faith in a future life.

What is most necessary is that a correct vision of what awaits them after death, of paradise especially, be given to the little ones.

"One day, as my little boy was taking the last bite of his ice cream cone," a lady told me, "he said to me without warning, 'Mommy, in heaven can a person have all the ice cream cones he wants?' Instead of answering him, I asked him in turn, 'What do you think heaven is?' 'A beautiful place where you really like it and you can have everything you want,' he answered. 'That's right, only when you get to heaven, everything you want will consist of being with God. You know that when you really like a person, you always want to be with that person. When your Mommy leaves you, you cry because you love her. You don't care about anything else. Do you remember the other day when Mark had to be left here with us because his mother had to stay with a sick relative? He was constantly crying. None of his toys, or the candy, or the stories we read made him feel better; they seemed unimportant compared to his mother. So, if during our lives we love God a lot, we won't be able to wait for the moment we can be with him.' 'Well then,' he cut in, 'heaven is better than ice cream.' "

Another mother explained the meaning of life and death to her children in this way: "Life consists in having Jesus grow in us to the point where Jesus finds himself so at home with our soul that he calls us to be with him always."

And here is how a father took advantage of circumstances to speak about death to his son: "Last summer we stayed in the mountains in a house belonging to some people there. They had a close relative who wasn't well and finally died. All the people of the area shared in the sorrow of the family. This seemed very unusual to us city dwellers and we talked about it quite a bit, even with the children. We came to feel that even though we didn't know the dead person well, he was our neighbor and we ought to participate in his funeral. And that's what we did. After the church services, my son John and I went to the cemetery with the funeral procession. It was almost a mile from the church. But the August evening was exceptionally beautiful. As we were going along, I spoke to John who was next to me. We talked about this very simple and human ceremony. At the cemetery, when the coffin was placed on the grave, the closest relative, and then all the others, threw a handful of earth on it — an ancient gesture. Everything was over.

"As we were returning home, John asked me questions about the meaning of what he had seen, especially about the value of various parts of the ceremony. 'Look, John,' I said, 'all these people are quite sad now. And did you see how much love and suffering they had as they followed the ceremony? Now some will say that it's over. That poor body will decay under the ground, and in a while who will remember it any more? But let's not forget what happened to the grain of wheat. Remember how this past winter we put a few grains of wheat in a vase and at a certain moment we saw a green shoot pop up? Remember what you said? That a new life had begun precisely because that little grain buried under the earth had decayed. When we buried it under the earth, it seemed finished; it seemed dead. But there was no death. There was always life, which then grew into a sprout and then into a blossoming plant that bore new grains of wheat. That's how it is for the body too. While the soul is alive in heaven, the body for now is under the earth and will decay. It seems dead, but as with the grain of wheat, here too is life, which will later rise up with the soul at the resurrection and that will be the true complete Life.' From the way he listened, it was obvious that John understood these things. They seemed logical to him, and he was happy with them. He was just like one who discovers something that corresponds to the deepest part of himself; he takes it all in, grasps it without any effort, and ends up enlightened and content."

Two mothers recounted the stories of how their children came in contact with death. This is what they told me:

"The first time my children were really affected by suffering related to death was when I was expecting my fourth child. All of us had been waiting very anxiously for him, but during the final months of pregnancy, things went wrong and it turned out that their little brother didn't make it. Soon, the children learned that death is a sorrowful separation because it divided us from the person we love. At the same time, they saw death as reuniting a child with the Father, as a real homecoming. As Dan my oldest son put it, while trying to console me at the time, 'When you think about it we already have a little brother in heaven. That's something beautiful, isn't it, Mommy?"

And the other mother: "John had his first encounter with death one evening after I received a phone call from a dear friend of mine who told me of her mother's death. It was a very short call. By returning to the dishes I was washing in the kitchen, I tried to hide my feelings. But John, who knows me very well, saw right away that I had been crying. 'Why are you crying?' he asked. 'Because Aida's mother has gone to paradise.' Well, he looked at me very surprised. 'Mommy, if she's gone to paradise, I don't see why you're crying!' 'Look,' I answered him, 'I'm not crying because she's gone to heaven but because I loved her very much and it'll be a long time before I'll see her again. And most of all, I'm sorry for Aunt Aida who was very close to her mother, and who has to wait a long time before seeing her again.' He saw the point right away: 'You're right, Mommy. We're happy because she's gone to heaven, but it's okay to cry too.'

"Last year, when John was seven, his grandfather (my father) died. He had spent a lot of time with us. We were in the midst of the Christmas season, and believed that the most beautiful Christmas Grandpa could have was this one in which he would meet God.

John understood that Grandpa's soul had gone to God, and that he was therefore having his own Christmas. Yet John had loved those hands that had often held and caressed him and those warm eyes that had looked so lovingly upon him. And he knew that the body of his grandfather was now in a casket buried under the ground. He had had seen the burial and it bothered him. I recall that when he brought his perplexity into the open, we were walking along a street lined with agave plants, sometimes called century plants. A thought came to me: 'Do you see how hardy this plant is, Johnny? It is said to live for one hundred years. After one hundred years, it produces a tall, beautiful flower; then the whole plant dies. If you look at the earth, you can see the destruction of this plant, for its leaves dry out and fall to the ground. If you look upward, you see a splendid flower. I think you can compare death to this. If we look at our souls, we see that we flower in heaven. If we look at our body, we see destruction. In order to let that flower go up to heaven, the body sacrifices itself, it dies. But all of this is part of a design of love, and for a good that is much greater.' "